For Oliver – D.H.
For my dad – K.W.

Sounds True
Boulder, CO 80306

Copyright © 2018 Deborah Hopkinson
Illustrations © 2018 Kailey Whitman

Published 2018
Book design by Lisa Kerans
Printed in China
Interior printed on FSC-compliant paper

Library of Congress Cataloging-in-Publication Data
Names: Hopkinson, Deborah, author. | Whitman, Kailey, illustrator.
Title: Under the Bodhi Tree : a story of the Buddha / by Deborah Hopkinson ;
    illustrated by Kailey Whitman.
Description: Boulder, CO : Sounds True, 2018. | Audience: Ages 4–8.
Identifiers: LCCN 2017056008 (print) | LCCN 2018002670 (ebook) |
    ISBN 9781683642497 (ebook) | ISBN 9781683641537 (hardcover)
Subjects: LCSH: Gautama Buddha]—Juvenile literature.
Classification: LCC BQ892 (ebook) | LCC BQ892 .H67 2018 (print) |
    DDC 294.3/63 [B]—dc23
LC record available at https://lccn.loc.gov/2017056008

10 9 8 7 6 5 4 3 2 1

Under the bodhi tree

a Story of the Buddha

Deborah Hopkinson

illustrations by Kailey Whitman

SOUNDS TRUE
many voices, one journey

In a long-ago time
and a faraway place,
a baby boy was born.

His name was Prince Siddhartha.

Before his birth,
his mother dreamed
of a beautiful white elephant.
The wise men said it was a sign
the baby would be special.

And he was.
Just like babies
then and now,
and everywhere.

And just like you.

The baby grew to be
a kind and gentle child.

Once, he found a wounded swan
and nursed it back to health
so it could soar
across the sky again.

The little prince wanted
to spread his wings, too.

But his father said,

"You must stay here,
away from the world,
where I can keep you safe
from any pain or sorrow."

And so Siddhartha grew up behind the garden walls
of a rich and splendid palace. He had new, fine clothes,
a grand white horse, the softest rice to eat.

But like children then and now, and everywhere, and just like you ...

he longed to
discover the world.

At last, when Siddhartha was a young man,
his father let him visit the great city.

The king ordered the mayor:
"Hold a festival in the market
with flowers, song, and dance.
My son must see only happy sights."

But, of course, the prince was curious
and wandered off to explore.
And that is how he first came to see
hardship, pain, and suffering.

First, he gave a sip of water
to a person lying sick with fever.

Next, he helped an old man
with an aching, crooked back
cross the road.

Then, he bowed his head
to share a grieving family's sorrow.

Siddhartha's heart felt
heavy and his own eyes
filled with tears. He could
not stop wondering:
How can I help others?

"You can do much good as a prince,"
the king told his troubled son.
Siddhartha shook his head.

"Even the wisest ruler cannot stop
sickness, old age, and death," he said.
"I want to find a way to help
people live in ease and peace."

And so, like seekers then and now,
and everywhere, the prince
set off to find his way,
just as you may
do someday.

At first, Siddhartha looked
to others for answers.
He journeyed far and long
and followed many different paths.

But he still felt lost,
like a little ship in a stormy sea,
tossed by wind and waves.

One day, Siddhartha
came upon the welcoming
shade of a tall, majestic tree.

His spirits rose and he thought,
Perhaps the answer is inside me.
I will stay in this pleasant grove
until I find a way to peace.
Then I can teach others, too.

And so Siddhartha crossed
his legs in quiet meditation.

Many days passed.
Raindrops fell.
Cool breezes blew.
The sun beat down.

And still Siddhartha sat,
sheltered by the rustling,
heart-shaped leaves
of the old and lovely tree.

Once, a woman named Sujata passed by
and thought, *He looks weak and hungry.*

She brought him sweetened milk and rice.
She smiled and said, "Please accept this gift.
If you are hungry, you should eat."

Siddhartha tipped back the bowl
to taste the delicious treat.
The rice and milk was warm and sweet!

"Thank you for your kindness," he said.

On that clear and brilliant night,
waves still rippled
the surface of his mind.
But now the prince just let
his fears and worries come and go
and kept on breathing mindfully,
in and out, deep and slow.

Soon, even the sighing,
heart-shaped leaves
grew still—
as serene as
Siddhartha's mind.

And then,
just before dawn,
he looked up.
In the eastern sky,
a bright planet appeared:
the morning star.

At that moment,
like the swan so long ago,
Siddhartha felt himself soar,
aware, free, and fully alive.
His worries fell away,
and he saw clearly
that all things fit together—
big and small,
hard and easy,
joyful and sad—

all part of one wondrous world.

In a time long ago
and a place far away,
a baby boy was born.
His name was Prince Siddhartha.

Today, we call him the Buddha,
the Awakened One.

Buddha did not stay alone
under the heart-shaped leaves
of the sacred Bodhi Tree.

Instead, he rose
and went into the world to
show the way of peace
to others…

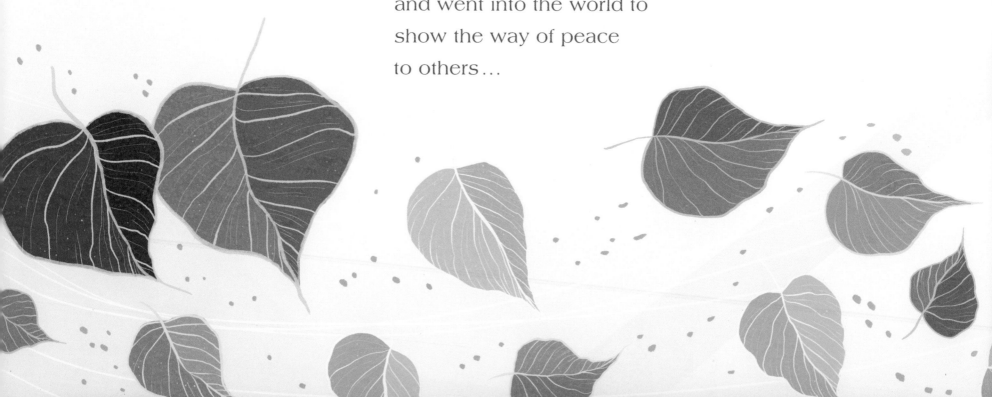

then and now,
and everywhere.

And yes, of course,
to you and me.

About the Buddha

Siddhartha Gautama, the boy who grew up to be called the Buddha, was indeed a real person. But he lived so long ago we can't even be certain of the dates of his life and death. Scholars believe Siddhartha was born in Lumbini, which was part of northern India in ancient times but is now in Nepal. It's said that Queen Maya, wife of a king or clan chief named Śuddhodana, gave birth probably sometime around 623 BCE. Buddha's birth is usually celebrated on April 8.

His mother died soon after his birth, and Siddhartha was raised by his father and his mother's sister, Mahapajapati. Stories about his life include the incident with the wounded swan, as well as his first encounters with sickness, old age, and death. It's also said that his beautiful white horse, Kanthaka, died of a broken heart when Siddhartha left home on his spiritual quest. By then, he was married to a cousin named Yasodharā and had a son, Rāhula.

Siddhartha explored yoga and other spiritual paths, including fasting from food. It's said that when he came to an ancient fig tree in Bodh Gaya, he vowed not to rise before attaining enlightenment. Scriptures include the story of Sujata bringing him a special rice milk pudding.

Since Buddha's time, the tree (*Ficus religiosa*) has become known as a Bodhi Tree. It has beautiful, heart-shaped leaves known for their constant swaying. At Bodh Gaya, there is a tree that pilgrims visit which is believed to be a descendent of that ancient sacred tree.

Buddha's teachings are called the *dharma* and focus on mindfulness, nonviolence, and compassion. The *sangha* is the community, which includes people the world over. Many Buddhist traditions include mindful breathing and meditation, which anyone can learn to do.

RAPID TRANSIT SYSTEMS

AND THE DECLINE OF STEAM

By Christopher Chant; edited by John Moore

Grange BOOKS

Published in 2002 by
Grange Books
An imprint of Grange Books Plc
The Grange
Kingsnorth Industrial Estate
Hoo, nr Rochester
Kent ME3 9ND
www.grangebooks.co.uk

ISBN 1 84013 359 7

Printed in Hong Kong

TITLE PAGE: *The Wuppertal monorail,
Germany.*

RIGHT: *A train on London's Docklands
Light Railway at Westferry.*

RAPID TRANSIT SYSTEMS AND THE DECLINE OF STEAM

One of the primary criticisms aimed at the steam locomotive right from its beginnings was the fact that as an engine it was manpower-intensive. A driver and fireman were both essential on the footplate for even the shortest trip, and large numbers of other staff were required throughout the entire railroad system to cope with matters such as coaling, watering, oiling and ash disposal. The beginning of the railroad era was a time in which manpower was both relatively abundant and relatively cheap, so these problems were initially not of major significance, but as time progressed and the world's railroad systems increased in extent and complexity, the manpower problem began to become more acute.

Long before the driver and fireman arrived to drive a steam locomotive, the latter's steam had to be raised and then maintained. Lying from cold, the average steam locomotive required at least four hours to reach its working pressure, and as a result burned a considerable (and increasingly expensive) quantity of high-quality coal before it even started to move and thus begin to generate revenue. A 1952 survey found that of the total weight of coal used by a 'Hall'-class 4-6-0 locomotive, designed and manufactured for the Great

Western Railway, more than one-fifth was burned in non-productive work including cleaning, the building-up of the fire, standing and manoeuvring.

A feature typical of railroad and railway systems all over the world was the sheer number of the engine sheds that were required right through the entire system, for these sheds were the 'bases' at which steam locomotives had to stand periodically for basic servicing of the types quoted above. A main-line engine would often be in steam for a week or more, but frequent washings of their boilers were essential if these essential parts of the whole locomotive system were not to 'fur up' and thus cease to work as efficiently as they might. The task of washing out the boiler required that the fire be dropped and the boiler emptied of water, for only after these had been completed could the maintenance crew embark on the filthy and incredibly laborious task of using hand tools to scrape away all the deposits that had accumulated in the boiler and the mass of tubes it contained. The task involved the use of rods and high-pressure water jets, inserted into the boiler through inspection holes, for the removal of the lime scale that had grown on the interior surfaces of the boiler and on its

tubes; if left, such lime scale increased the weight of the locomotive to an appreciable extent, reduced the overall efficiency of the boiler system, and as a result seriously degraded the ability of the steam locomotive to operate both well and economically. Another aspect of the servicing procedure was the removal of as much as possible of the dirt that collected in other parts of the workings of the steam locomotive, whose performance and operating economy were also highly dependent on the type of mechanical cleanliness that could be ensured, and then only to a strictly limited degree, by the removal of deposits of ash and clinker from the firebed, ash from the pan, soot from the interior of the boiler tubes, and char from the smokebox: if left, all of these had a major effect for the worse on the ability of the steam locomotive to generate and use its steam economically.

Routine maintenance was also needed on items such as valves and pistons, together with other parts of the steam locomotive's workings requiring lubrication. This somewhat cleaner aspect of maintenance combined with the dirty aspects of the task as mentioned above to make the operation of a steam locomotive

much more manpower-intensive and therefore more expensive than any other type of motive power during the 19th century. The manpower-intensive and time-consuming nature of steam locomotive operations is perhaps encapsulated in the small but significant fact that while modern trains can be driven from either end, trains pulled by steam locomotives are essentially single-ended, so the locomotive had to be uncoupled at the end of a journey and turned round before it could be coupled to the return service: this task required the attentions of several men, and generally took between one and two hours.

The cost in terms of manpower and time was only one aspect of steam locomotive operations that came to militate against their continued use as and when alternatives began to become available. Another aspect of steam locomotive operations that gradually began to assume increasing importance was their essentially anti-social nature, and this fact began to gain significance from the beginning of the 20th century to peak, in the Western world, during the 1950s. In short, increasing national affluence and an expanding awareness of the ideas of better working conditions and the desirability of greater

RIGHT: Part of the problem of steam locomotion is neatly encapsulated in this photograph of typical double-headed steam railway operations. Although the white steam appears clean, in fact it is full of particulate matter, especially when those parts are mixed with smoke, and as a result all elements of railroad operation were grimy, and this grime also spread to neighbouring buildings.

leisure time meant that dirty, manual tasks such as the maintenance and operation of steam locomotives gradually became something to be avoided wherever possible: thus the crews of steam locomotives, who had been among the heroes of the Victorian era and feted in numberless songs, acquired during the 20th century something of the pariah among the working classes as men condemned to dirty and laborious employment that generally took them far from home on long shifts. The effect of this process was to reduce the pool of skilled and industrious manpower from which steam locomotive driving and maintenance crews could be drawn, and as a result the overall standard of these crews became increasingly difficult to maintain. Although this tendency was most readily appreciable in the wealthier countries of the Western world, it also began to appear (albeit later and more slowly) in Latin American countries and also in many Third World nations, where the adherence to the concept of the steam locomotive was seen not as a reflection of the success and economic viability of the existing system when the adoption of 'modern technology' might cost much in both capital and operating terms, but rather as further evidence that the

nations of the Third World were being kept deliberately in the past as a reflection of the First World's belief that they were inferior and therefore incapable of buying and using 'modern technology'. As recently as 1982, a Brazilian report on the continued operation of the Teresa Cristina Railway suggested that steam locomotives should be replaced by more modern diesel or electric locomotives as soon as possible, as the retention of steam power was undesirable for reasons as diverse as the tendency of the steam locomotive's crews to suffer from high levels of stress, high levels of vibration as a result of the workings of the locomotive and the unevenness of track, hearing loss as a result of the high levels of noise, a tendency toward infection as a result of the 'thermal overload' to which the crews were often subjected, a tendency toward back problems later in life as a result of the work, a tendency toward lung disease as a result of the coal dust, and a tendency toward loss of sight as a result of the brightness of the light coming from the firebox.

Many of these factors were obviously unjustified or, where justified, somewhat exaggerated, but the report in general highlighted the increasing unrest felt by the

LEFT: A newcomer in electric train operations in 1906 was this Baldwin-Westinghouse-built locomotive designed to operate on both direct and alternating current (direct current over the New York Central line and alternating current on New Haven's own line). This type of locomotive was capable of handling a 200-ton train in local service at an average speed of 26mph (42km/h). The maximum speed travelled to maintain this average speed was about 45mph (72km/h).

OPPOSITE: Whatever its failings, steam locomotion nevertheless possesses a unique emotional appeal, and even when the country through which the railroad passes has been raped for the construction of tunnels and cuttings, as seen here in the Cumbria region of north-west England, nature is quick to re-establish itself. This is one of the reasons why preserved railroad operations have proved so enduringly popular.

persons who were still maintaining and driving steam locomotives at a time when the operation of diesel or electric locomotives was clearly coming to be seen as a far cleaner and less laborious option, better suited to the dignity and long-term well-being of the modern working man.

In these circumstances, therefore, the change to diesel and electrical locomotives was in general the subject of an enthusiastic welcome by the members of a work force that had become increasingly disenchanted

with the steam locomotive and all the work and discomfort that its operation entailed. Unlike the steam locomotive, which is wholly reliant on the movement of large quantities of coal, first from the reserves in the depot into the tender (often by mechanical means) and then from the tender to the firebox (most generally by shovel), the diesel locomotive uses an easily transportable liquid fuel that is loaded into the locomotive's fuel tanks and from there to the burners by mechanical means. The

diesel fuel also possesses the advantages of being consistent in its qualities, lacking the waste products that would choke the operating system and, most importantly of all for the locomotive's crew, having no need for the disposal of wastes after use. Another point in favour of the diesel locomotive, so far as the operating company as well as the crew are concerned, is that while the steam locomotive needs a full head of steam before reaching its maximum operating capability, a costly and time-

consuming process, as noted above, the diesel locomotive is free from this stricture. The same is also true of the electric locomotive, and as a result neither of these types requires any significant measure of 'warm up' time, with consequent saving in fuel and labour costs, and for the same reason provide greater tractive effort on gradients and during acceleration.

The most cogent argument against the use of steam locomotives was the need for huge weights of coal to be transported from

the various coal-mining regions to strategically placed dumps serving the railroad industry. Sometimes countries and railroad operators were fortunate that deposits of the right grade of coal were located close to major industrial regions, which of course grew up where the raw materials (including coal) for their operations were most readily available, but in others railroad systems were only partially co-located with their fuel supplies, especially where there was already a thriving economic life based on other aspects of transports such as shipping, for instance. What could not be avoided, however, was the fact that large-scale railroad systems required large coal dumps located at about one tender's steaming distance from each other. The primary disadvantages of such dumps were, on the one hand, that they had to be maintained with frequent deliveries of coal and in themselves demanded large numbers of men for the movement of the coal and, on the other hand, needed very large areas of increasingly expensive land. The beautiful irony of this coal situation was, naturally, that the delivery of coal to these dumps demanded an extensive schedule of transport by trains hauled by a coal-burning steam locomotive. The movement of coal in the required tonnages was a major task, but speed of delivery was not vitally important and as a result the coal-delivery trains were among the longest, heaviest but slowest to be encountered on any railroad system. The coal-delivering trains generally operated at night, together with most of the other freight services, to avoid daylight congestion of a system that was most profitably employed during the day for passenger and light freight services.

Not just any type of coal was suitable for use in steam locomotives, which worked to best effect only with the high-quality coal mined only in a limited number of areas. In the United Kingdom, for example, it was the coal from the collieries of South Wales that was thought the best for steam locomotion, and this coal offered a 13 per cent better return, in terms of steam generated per unit of coal, than the coal mined in Yorkshire. It was this factor that required the movement of large tonnages of coal so that the fuel for steam locomotives would be available in areas in which it was not mined. The cost of this movement of coal was just one of the many factors that began to militate against the continued use of coal in the first half of the 20th century, and another was the notably rapid exhaustion of the best reserves of high-quality coal. This meant greater costs as less accessible deposits were exploited, and also reduced operating efficiency as many operators switched to coal of reduced quality in an effort to cut direct costs. Thus it was the combination of the increasing shortage and increased cost of high-quality coal with the availability of oil that was both plentiful and comparatively cheap that led to the demise of the steam locomotive in the Western world. The comparative costs of steam and diesel locomotion in the early 1950s, measured in terms of pence per mile,

were about 36 pence for the coal-fired locomotive and 11 pence for the diesel-engined locomotive, which was thus more than three times cheaper to operate than the steam locomotive. Another aspect that was inevitably and correctly factored into the notional equation concerning the cost-effectiveness of the diesel-powered locomotive vis-à-vis the steam locomotive is that the former is generally available for service for about 90 per cent of its life, while the latter has far greater 'down' periods.

As noted above, a major factor that boosted the change from steam to other forms of locomotive power was the anti-social nature, either real or imaginary, of the work associated with the steam locomotive. The driver and firemen of steam locomotives had of necessity to work in conditions that were both dirty and arduous, whereas the drivers (the firemen now being superfluous) of diesel and electric locomotives were favoured with a far more user-friendly environment in cabs that were sealed from the weather and radically cleaner than the cabs of steam locomotives.

Another aspect of the switch from steam to diesel locomotion – and this was an aspect that became increasingly important to the populations of Western nations as the 20th century progressed – was the fact that such locomotives were considerably more friendly to the environment than the steam locomotives they replaced. There was less smoke and no steam to act as pollutants of the air, and as a

consequence there were clear advantages in overall terms as well as in smaller specifics such as the cleanliness of buildings and the reduced irritation to the eyes, lungs and skins of people living near the railway, which was in fact an omnipresent feature of urban life by the beginning of the 20th century: the exhaust gases of the steam locomotive contain acids that get into people's lungs and also coat and then etch their way into the stonework of buildings. In this regard it is worth noting that most of the cities and larger towns of the Western world were virtually black with the deposits of steam locomotives by the middle of the 20th century, and it was only after these engines had been replaced by diesel and electric locomotives that it made economic

ABOVE: *With their abundant supplies of coal, lack of pressure from environmental and customer lobbies, and unwillingness to invest in new technology when there was still mileage to be had from the existing system, the communist regimes of Europe were slow to abandon steam locomotion, with the result that engines were still being built or, increasingly, rebuilt right into the 1970s as indicated by this photograph taken in Czechoslovakia during 1975.*

OPPOSITE: *SY1422 with bankers JS 6217 and 6218 on the Chengde Steelworks branch, China.*

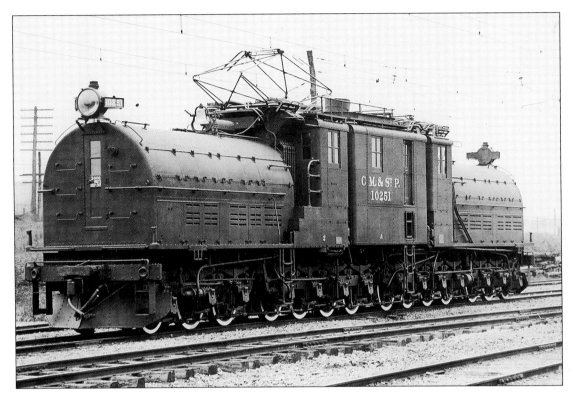

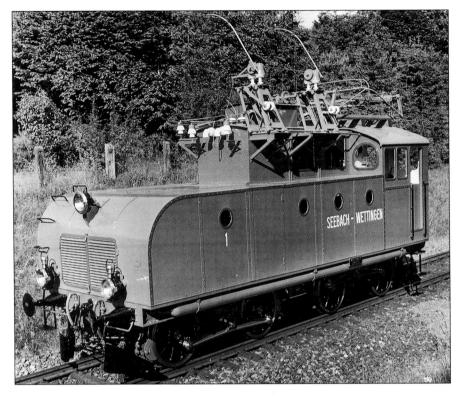

ABOVE: *Chicago, Milwaukee & St. Paul Railroad Class 6886-E-12GE100A electric locomotive.*

ABOVE RIGHT: *Swiss Federal Railways Seebach-Wettingen locomotive Ce 4/41 Eva, 1904.*

OPPOSITE: *Fast freight train on the Baltimore & Ohio Railroad's Susquehanna river bridge at Havre de Grace, Maryland.*

sense to undertake the extensive programmes of cleaning and restoration that have once more revealed the fact that many buildings, once thought to be entirely indifferent, are in fact magnificent bequests from the past.

Electrification is an extremely costly process in the initial stages, when equipment had to be installed and electricity-generating capability built. This is in general a one-off capital cost, however, and is supportable when the result is a system offering the assurance of high-density movement of passengers and/or freight. Where such a 'market' is thought to be available, most notably in the regions surrounding large conurbations or

connecting major cities, it makes sense to proceed with electrification on the basis of a comparatively few electricity-generating stations of high capacity located strategically to feed power to the electric motors of locomotives by means of overhead wires or a conducting rail on the ground. This allows the use of simpler and therefore cheaper locomotives that do not need to generate their own power, but is viable in economic terms only when there is a high level of traffic. In areas offering a lower level of traffic, it makes greater economic sense to reduce the capital outlay required by forsaking the concept of an external power source and instead rely on the slightly greater operating cost

associated with on-board generation of power through the use of either a diesel powerplant or a diesel-electric generating system.

It is worth noting, however, that diesel and electric power have not replaced or indeed largely supplanted steam locomotion in every country. Up to a time within the last ten years, India was still seen as the world's second most important 'steam country' after China, and to a large extent the railroad systems of the two nations reflected two radically different approaches to steam locomotion: in 1990 China was operating some 8,000 steam locomotives, of a mere six classes, while India had considerably smaller numbers of engines

but of a far larger variety of classes.

The Indian railroad system was also based on the continued use of steam locomotion on tracks of four different gauges. Then the nature of the Indian railroad system was radically overhauled, and by 1997 India's use of steam locomotion had been radically curtailed. Even as the Indian railways organization was undertaking its long-term programme of progressive modernization, the national feeling against the continuance of steam locomotion, in emotive as well as practical terms, was strengthening. Steam locomotion had now effectively disappeared from the wide-gauge railroad system, leaving for extinction by the beginning of the 21st century only the surviving pockets of steam locomotion on the metre-gauge track system currently represented by the 'YP'-class 'Pacific'-type and 'YG'-class 'Mikado'-type locomotives. On the narrow-gauge track system, 1997 saw the advent of diesel locomotives on the previous steam line from Pulgaon to Arvi, this leaving only the 24-inch (610-mm) gauge Matheran and the famous Darjeeling lines, both of them used mainly for the tourist trade rather than for more practically oriented commercial purposes, with steam locomotion: even so, financial requirements imposed by the government of India mean that even the Darjeeling Himalayan 'toy railroad' is now threatened. Completed in 1889, the railroad climbs its way for some 50 miles (80km) from the flat lands of West Bengal up to Darjeeling in a beautiful location some 7,250ft (2210m) above sea level. The

LEFT: Locomotive No. 797 on the local line from Kurseong to Darjeeling below Sonada, India.

OPPOSITE: Narrow-gauge steam railroads are still of importance in remoter and less accessible parts of the world, for here the amount of traffic makes it very problematical whether or not the financial return will justify the expense of new locomotives, rolling stock and infrastructure.

current situation of the railroad is appalling, with stations in need of repairs, carriages requiring restoration and tracks in need of maintenance lest they subside, and the only real chance for the railroad's survival is the Darjeeling Himalayan Railway Heritage Foundation, which is seeking to save the line by developing it as a major tourist attraction.

Oddly enough, however, the railroad-minded visitor to India will fortunately discover the fact that there have been a number of fascinating survivals on the wide-gauge system, most of these relics being associated with industrial service. These hangovers from the past include a heavy 0-8-4 hump shunter and the last examples of the great 'XE' class of 2-8-2 locomotives. These are the only units left in

OPPOSITE: YB 534 goods train from Mottama nearing Tha Ton, Myanmar (Burma).

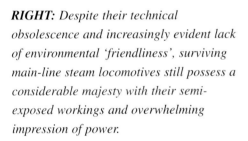

RIGHT: Despite their technical obsolescence and increasingly evident lack of environmental 'friendliness', surviving main-line steam locomotives still possess a considerable majesty with their semi-exposed workings and overwhelming impression of power.

the world of large, classically styled British Mikado-type locomotives and, at 200 tons, are the final examples of the big British steam locomotive left in service anywhere in the world. Toward the other end of the size scale, the most fascinating aspects of steam locomotion to survive in India are employed in the sugar field railroads of the country's northern regions. In one of the paradoxes so beloved by nature, it is here in a country that has now disposed of virtually all of its active steam locomotives that there are the world's two oldest steam locomotives still in active service. These are

the metre-gauge 0-4-0 type locomotives named as the *Mersey* and *Tweed*: the engines were manufactured in 1873 by the Great Bridgewater Street Works of Sharp Stewart.

In Pakistan, India's north-western neighbour, the national railroad organization's core is provided by the 66-inch (1676-mm) track system using British steam locomotives designed at the start of the 20th century, most notably inside-cylinder 0-6-0 and 4-4-0 type locomotives. Bangladesh (East Pakistan up to 1971) is India's north-eastern neighbour but has

little more than the remnants of a railroad system, so it is in Myanmar (formerly Burma), farther to the east, that one can find further railroad remnants of the original British presence in the Indian subcontinent. Virtually closed to foreigners for almost two decades and still difficult to visit, Myanmar has a small but fascinating collection of old British steam locomotives. Despite the fact that there are fewer than 50 examples left in service, these locomotives are of three important British-derived classes, all of them standard designs of the Indian railways organization during the

1920s: after the retirement of India's last 'YP'-class metre-gauge locomotives, the 'YB'- and 'YC'-class locomotives are the world's last Pacific-type locomotives still in service.

With about 5,000 steam locomotives in active service, despite a fall of 3,000 from the peak figure of 8,000 in 1990 – still a number greater than the rest of the world put together, China is the most important country so far as steam locomotion is concerned. Despite the sheer numbers of steam locomotives in service, however, it is a disappointment to the railroad enthusiast

ABOVE: Locomotive HGS 2306 on Khyber *stands at Shahgai Station, the Khyber Pass, on the Afghanistan/Pakistan border.*

ABOVE RIGHT: Engine SPS 2976 en route between Mithalak and Malakwal, on the Dorridge Special *from Sargodha, Pakistan.*

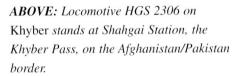

OPPOSITE: YC 630 passing Payagyi station on the double-track main line between Bago and Pyuntaza, Myanmar.

that this total comprises only three types. This is the result of the fact that China, as a communist state, is a firm adherent of the concept of centralized planning without competition from commercial organizations, and this makes extensive standardization both logical and easy. This standardization also derives from the fact that much of China's railroad system was destroyed in World War II and the following Chinese Civil War, so it was only after the establishment of communist rule in 1949 that rebuilding of the system, together with its locomotives and rolling stock, could be undertaken. The absence of much pre-war equipment thus made the communists' centralized planning concept that much more attractive.

In numerical terms the world's most important steam locomotive, the 'QJ'-class locomotive is of the 2-10-2 type, and is partnered on Chinese main-line services by the 'JS' class of lighter Mikado-type locomotive. The most important class of steam locomotive for industrial purposes is the 'SY' class of Mikado-type locomotives to a design basically similar to that of the American 'light Mike' of the period before World War II. In the later part of the 1970s, China achieved considerable international note by the revelation that it was still manufacturing steam locomotives. Such was the pace of this effort, indeed, that there were occasions during the 1980s when the Datong Locomotive Works, located on the border with Inner Mongolia,

was completing one QJ-class locomotive every day.

Construction of steam locomotives has now almost entirely ended, reflecting a radical shift in emphasis within the communist system: the central government's plan that steam locomotives should be the norm was stymied when China's separate railway bureaux achieved a measure of autonomy and stopped their purchase of such locomotives as they opted for major modernizations of their systems. The change reflected partially a desire for greater operational efficiency, and also in part a revulsion, if that is not too strong a word, against steam on environmental and emotional grounds. Thus the Chinese railroad situation in the last years of the

20th century is akin to that which held sway in the Western world during the 1950s and 1960s, where there was a wholesale swing away from steam locomotion in favour of diesel and electric power.

Even so, the manufacturing facility at Tangshan is still delivering about one SY-class 2-8-2 locomotive every month, generally for industrial purposes and particularly for the coal-mining industry: by the end of the 20th century nearly 1,750 SY-class locomotives had been delivered. The Chinese are also happy, for the obvious commercial reasons that have become more important to the communists in the 1990s, to manufacture steam locomotives for state railways and also for tourist lines, and as a result Tangshan has already produced a small number of Mikado-type locomotives for Vietnam as well as a few SY-class locomotives for preserved railways in the U.S.A.

The most significant highlight in the Chinese retention of steam locomotives is the network of provincial lines that are not an intrinsic part of the state system. Developed with local financing, these railroads cannot generally run to the purchase and operating costs of diesel locomotives, and certainly not to those of electric locomotives, so they seem likely candidates for the retention of steam power until a time well after the disappearance of steam locomotives from the state system. Together with a declining number of industrial operators such as the coal, iron, stone, forestry and manufacturing industries, these provincial railroads are

ABOVE: China's first electric railway opens to traffic. People gave a warm send-off to the first electric locomotive when it pulled out of the Chengtu station on 1 July 1975.

ABOVE RIGHT: China's first electric railway running from Paoki in Shensi to Chengtu in Szechwan. A passenger train is travelling through the mountains pulled by an electric locomotive.

RIGHT: Although it is declining in importance, steam locomotion is still very important to China for tasks such as logging.

OPPOSITE: Majestic 6991 and 6898 locomotives on the Jing Peng line, climbing over a curving viaduct with east-bound goods.

planning to retain steam power for many years into the future. Indeed, in the case of the narrow-gauge railroad lines used for forestry work with standard 0-8-0 type locomotives of both European and Chinese origin, a not inconsiderable number of new steam locomotives was introduced during the 1980s.

In overall terms, therefore, it seems likely that steam locomotives will remain important to certain elements of the Chinese railroad system to at least 2015. This is a pleasant thought for those fascinated by steam power, for it will mean the use of steam locomotives for more than 200 years before their disappearance as first-line equipment. However, it should not be ignored that steam locomotives had disappeared from China's national railroad network by 1995.

The situation in North Korea, China's eastern neighbour, is basically similar to that in China, and thus a measure of steam locomotion remains for service on non-electrified lines and for shunting duties. The situation with the steam locomotive equipment of the North Korean railroad system is somewhat obscure, as a result largely of the closed nature of this most centralized and introspective member of the world's declining number of communist states; but it is thought that there are still many types of steam locomotive still in existence if not actually in operational service. North Korea is well provided with deposits of high-quality coal but is sorely vexed in overall financial terms, so it is likely that locomotives such as ex-American

'S160'-class 2-8-0 locomotives and 0-6-0T-type units will continue to be seen alongside ex-Chinese 'JF'- and 'JF6'-class Mikado-type locomotives.

The most fascinating exemplar of the countries that still retain steam locomotion is Indonesia (The Dutch East Indies until shortly after World War II), especially the large island of Java. For its size, this island had until the late 1970s one of the most varied but also most aged fleets of steam locomotives anywhere in the world. Although most of the island's main railroad lines are now the home of more modern diesel locomotives, steam locomotives had nonetheless survived in large numbers in association with the island's huge sugar industry, whose great sugar-cane plantations are still dotted with a large assortment of steam locomotives, some of them in working order but others in a state of total disrepair.

The origins of Indonesia as a Dutch colony is reflected, inevitably, in the presence of locomotives mostly of European, particularly Dutch and German, origins. If one had to sum up the relationship between Java and Europe in terms of the former's steam locomotion, the most apposite counterpart elsewhere in the world would be that of Cuba and the United States, the former being the last stronghold of the latter's steam heritage.

The steam locomotives of the Javanese agricultural system may be old and, when broken down, difficult to repair, but in overall commercial terms paid for themselves at a time well into the past and

are now operating at a virtually total profit, especially as their fireboxes burn bagasse, the natural and wholly free waste product of sugar-cane processing. On Sumatra, the large island to the east of Java, an equivalent situation prevails in the palm-oil processing, where the palm-oil plantations used steam locomotives whose boilers are heated by nutshells which are, again, a free by-product of the processing operation.

There is not much of the once extensive steam locomotion effort still evident in the Philippines except on the island of Negros, where there are still a number of sugar-plantation lines operated by small steam locomotives. A notable system of this type is the Hawaiian Philippine Sugar Company's 36-inch (914-mm) network

ABOVE and OPPOSITE: A 700mm-gauge 0-8-0 No.2 of 1913 shunting cane wagons in Java.

which has seven Baldwin locomotives known locally as 'Dragons'. As in Java, the Hawaiian Philippine locomotives burn bagasse through most of the sugar-cane season except the first weeks, when oil is burned until there are sufficient stocks of bagasse to allow a switch to this free fuel.

The other home in South-East Asia of steam locomotion as a significant factor is Vietnam, where steam locomotives survive both on the main lines and for industrial purposes. Although there are only a relatively few steam locomotives in daily service, a number of Mikado-type units operate on the country's metre-gauge and standard-gauge lines. Steam locomotives are most prevalent on the main lines to the south of the capital, Hanoi. In overall terms, the Vietnamese railroad organization is desperately hampered by an overactive bureaucracy, low wages, and lack of foreign exchange for the improvement of the situation with imported equipment. In combination with the lingering effects of the Vietnam War that ended in 1975 after the railway system had been very badly damaged, however, this is a situation that effectively guarantees the survival of steam locomotion for some time into the future.

An ex-French colony, Vietnam is also of significance as one of the last areas in the world with locomotives of the French school of thought, a type that is otherwise virtually extinct. However, the standard-gauge locomotives of the 2-8-2 type are of the Chinese 'JF' class and as such are especially important as some of the last examples of the classic American Mikado

LEFT: *Locomotive 141-199 leaving Du Nghia with the* Dorridge Special *to Haiphong, Vietnam.*

OPPOSITE: *A GP6 2-8-2 locomotive No. 1040 at Bacgiang Station with the* Dorridge Special, *Kep to Hanoi and Yên Vien, Vietnam.*

type, which has all but disappeared in China.

The very great majority of African railways was built under European colonial rule, or at least inspired by European thinking and often financed with European capital. Under these circumstances it is hardly surprising that almost all of the steam locomotives and rolling stock used on the continent's railroads were imported, mostly from the United Kingdom as a direct

consequence of the British predominance in colonial and economic affairs during the 19th century.

The importance of industry in South Africa was responsible for elevating this country to the position of the continent's greatest exponent of steam power to the extent that until recent years, and a thorough-going modernization of the South African railroad system, it was one of the most important elements in the worldwide

survival of steam locomotion. What cannot be denied now, however, is that the declining importance of railroads to South Africa and the overhaul of the system have signally reduced the importance of steam locomotion to the extent that its only surviving centres, already under threat, are the gold-mining and coal-mining industries.

Zimbabwe (formerly Rhodesia), South Africa's north-eastern neighbour, was until very recently the 'Land of the Garratt' as

some 90 per cent of the country's steam locomotives were of this type. Since that time, though, steam locomotion has been largely supplanted by diesel locomotion, though a small number of British-manufactured Garratt locomotives survive on shunting and tripping duties around Bulawayo. To the east of Zimbabwe on the coast of Africa to the south of Tanzania, Mozambique also has a small number of steam locomotives still in service.

On the other side of the African continent Ghana, once a perfect example of the British railway concept translated to a colonial setting, again has no steam locomotion left, a fact that is made all the more poignant by the fact that the move away from a railway capability ignored British pleas for the retention of at least part of the country's steam heritage.

Farther to the north and east, steam locomotion is still evident in two countries,

namely Sudan and Eritrea. Despite its ethnic, religious and financial problems as well as the civil war of recent decades, Sudan had tried to maintain its excellent railway system together with at least some of the British-manufactured steam locomotives working on it. In Eritrea, a former Italian colony, there are efforts to recreate the main-line railroad connecting Massawa, Asmara and Agordat, which was closed in 1974 and has suffered years of

damage in the war with Ethiopia. If the railroad is in fact brought back into service, it is likely that these services will be hauled by renovated 0-4-4-0 Mallet tank engines built by the Ansaldo company of Italy during the 1930s.

Like Africa, Latin America at one time possessed some of the most exciting and varied steam railroad systems anywhere in the world, but is now falling prey to more modern thinking and a general contraction of railroad capabilities. The most important exception to this general tendency is Paraguay, which operates the last entirely steam-hauled main-line service in the world between Asunción, the national capital, and Encarnación, a town almost on the Argentine border. This classic railroad was slowly recovering a measure of life from 1997, following an earlier cessation of traffic, and one of the features of the line is the continued use of a number of Edwardian wood-burning 'Mogul'-type locomotives, built by North British of Glasgow. The railroad's maintenance works are located in the village of Sapucay and are in effect a working museum with all its equipment steam-driven through belts in classic 19th-century fashion. By contrast with Paraguay, Uruguay has disposed of its fleet of British locomotives, including the world's last 4-4-4T-type locomotives built by the Vulcan Iron Foundry of Newton-le-Willows in 1915, deemed redundant to a railroad system radically scaled down in favour of roads.

In Argentina little remains, although Henschel 2-8-2-type steam locomotives

survive on the 29.5-inch (750-mm) gauge Esquel branch. Argentina's other railroad of the same gauge is in the far south, extending from Rio Gallegos to Rio Turbio, and for its coal-carrying services the current force of Mitsubishi 2-10-2 type locomotives are being replaced by diesel locomotives. The industrial railways of Brazil have proved a treasure house of discovery in recent years, but few are now believed to operate steam locomotives. One other limited stronghold of steam locomotion in Latin America is Bolivia, where some former Argentine 2-8-2 and 4-6-0 type locomotives have made an unexpected return to steam working, especially for shunting.

Cuba has a secure niche in railroad history as the final stronghold of U.S. steam power, in this instance of the middle period of American steam locomotion with no locomotives dating from the period before 1878. The primary reason for the survival of steam locomotion in Cuba was the advent to power in 1959 of the regime headed by Fidel Castro, who soon fell out with the U.S.A. in a process that saw the virtual end of trade with any but the communist-bloc countries. For the steam enthusiast this is a blessing, for if the revolution had not occurred, American commercial interests, wholly predominant in Cuban life, would have pressed for rapid dieselization.

Although most of the locomotives operated on Cuba were built specifically for the island, some are ex-American railroad units. As a result, the Cuban register of

LEFT: *A massive Beyer-Garratt locomotive No. 4065, built by Henschel in 1954, at Rosmead, South Africa.*

BELOW: *Locomotive No. 4065 climbing from Jagpoort to Lootsberg.*

OPPOSITE: *Paraguayan steam railroad operations may appear decidedly rustic, but retain some of the classics of steam locomotion still serving a useful purpose in the closing stages of the 20th century.*

steam locomotives includes all the great American steam locomotive manufacturers such as Alco, Baldwin, Davenport, H.K. Porter, Rogers and the Vulcan Iron Foundry, whose designs are represented by a range of engines from 0-4-0 and 0-6-0 type saddle-tank engines to 2-6-0 type 'Mogul', 2-6-2 'Prairie' and 2-8-0 type locomotives. There are also a limited number of 4-6-0 locomotives as well as a few 2-4-2T and 0-4-4T engines.

Cuba has a great variety of gauges, including oddities such as 27-inch (686-mm), 34-inch (864-mm) and 36-inch (914-mm) gauges as well as 24-inch (610-m), 30-in (762-mm) and standard

gauges, and as a result there is very little interchange between the different systems, although an exception is a number of the standard-gauge networks which connect with the state railway's main lines. This fact makes it possible for sugar-mill trains to run (often for distances of 15 miles/24km or more) as 'main-line' trains where the distances from the cane fields to the factory requires through running. Another example of extensive working over the state system is the Fructuosa Rodriguez sugar mill, which undertakes round trips of 37 miles (60km).

Even in Cuba steam locomotion is now threatened, for the Soviets delivered a not

inconsiderable number of diesel locomotives for both the standard- and narrow-gauge railroad systems.

In global terms, the steam locomotive was gradually supplemented and then replaced in main-line service by the diesel-engined or electrically-powered locomotive within the context of a process that also saw the gradual but widespread advent of what are currently designated rapid-transit systems. These systems were specifically intended for the rapid delivery of passengers within the great cities of the period, which then became the bases for today's vast conurbations. The first rapid-transit systems were based conceptually on

the tramway, whose origins can be traced back to the plateways used in mines and quarries to ease the passage of horse-drawn wagons. The first street tramway to be introduced in a city was the New York & Harlem line of 1832. This led to the coining of the American term 'street railway', which is still in use. The world's second horse tramway, constructed during 1835 in New Orleans, is still in use today after a continuous history of more than 150 years, a remarkable testimony to the sound basic nature of the concept even though the services are now operated by electric cars. Crowning the efforts of American promoters, the tramway reached Europe in 1853 with the inauguration of the Paris system, and seven years later the first British system of this type was operational in Birkenhead. During 1861 the first section of London's network was opened, and the British capital was followed in 1963 by Copenhagen, the Danish capital.

The boom time for the construction of horse tramways was the 1870s, but even by this time the very real limitations of animal power had become apparent, and advocates of the tramway concept soon turned to the idea of mechanical power. Initial consideration was given to steam power, which was already very successful for railroad use, but though steam trams were developed and put into operation on many suburban and rural light railways, it was clear from the very beginning that steam power was ill-suited to urban applications. Other power sources, such as compressed air, gas and petrol engines were evaluated

LEFT: A 2-6-0 1510, manufactured by Alco in 1907, shunting at the Boris Luis Santa Coloma Mill, Cuba.

OPPOSITE LEFT: BLW 2-6-0 1531 on FCC tracks from José Smith Comas Mill, Cuba.

OPPOSITE RIGHT: The standard-gauge side of Osvaldo Sanchez Mill with a 2-4-2T 1204 (Rogers 1894) and a 4107 Whitcombe 40053-class 25DM18 gasoline-electric, photographed in Cuba.

with little success, and cable tramways enjoyed considerable success for a time. The most successful of the latter was that in San Francisco, where it is still used. All of these tractive methods were either mechanically unreliable or economically unrealistic, and rapidly became secondary after electric traction had become feasible.

The first electric vehicles were battery-powered, but in 1879 a German, Werner von Siemens, demonstrated his new type of practical dynamo. This was clearly the way ahead for electric traction using electricity generated at a fixed station and transmitted to its user by a conducting rail or overhead

wire. The first electric tramway for public use was opened in Berlin during 1881 by Siemens & Halske, and used a 180-volt current fed through the running rails. The first lines of this type in the U.K. were the Portrush & Bushmills (later Giant's Causeway) Tramway in Northern Ireland and Volk's Railway at Brighton in 1883, of which the latter is still operational.

Electrified running rails were not suitable for street use as a result of their safety considerations, so a change was made to overhead wires of the type first used on the Bessbrook & Newry line in Ireland in 1885. A slotted overhead tube was trialled in Paris during 1881, and other European cities with street railways included Frankfurt, which opened in 1884 and now possesses the lengthiest period of non-stop electric street tramway operation anywhere in the world: Frankfurt also used the slotted overhead tube system initially, but in 1906 switched to the more conventional overhead wire.

As they did not need poles and overhead wires, underground conduits were sometimes preferred as an alternative to overhead current collection where aesthetic considerations were thought to predominate over the practical aspects of tramway

operation: such a system was used in London until the end of tramway operations in 1952, and in Washington, D.C. until 1962. The U.K.'s oldest street tramway is that along the front at Blackpool, and has operated on an overhead system since 1899 although it made use of the conduit system when it was inaugurated during 1885.

Experience soon revealed that the overhead wire with trolley pole collection was without doubt the most practical solution to the problem of delivering electric power to a tramway car, and the first city tramway system of this type was created in Richmond, Virginia, during 1887. By 1900, almost all of the original American horse tramways had been adapted for electric traction, and Europe was not far behind the U.S.A. in this respect. In another striking piece of evidence to his technical expertise, Siemens developed the bow collector as an alternative to the trolley pole and this in turn led to the pantograph which is today the most frequently-used method of collecting electrical power from an overhead line. Before the end of the 19th century, electric tramways were common in many parts of the world including the Australian city of Melbourne, the Japanese city of Kyoto and the Siamese city of Bangkok. British tramways in the U.K., and also in those parts of the world in which the British influence was strongest, generally opted for double-decked trams as a means of maximizing capacity without creating a larger footprint. On the mainland of Europe, a single-deck tram towing a trailer was more common, and in the U.S.A. larger trams mounted on two bogies soon became the norm.

The golden age of the tramway is generally regarded to have been the first quarter of the 20th century: virtually every major city operated such a system, most of the systems under municipal control rather than private ownership. As well as offering cheap and reliable transport for the masses, the tramway also played a major part in the relevant city's economic development

OPPOSITE: A Norwegian State Railways Class El 16 electric locomotive heading a passenger train.

RIGHT: A Class 20 electric locomotive alongside a Class 800 EMU (electric motor unit) of Belgian State Railways, late 1970s.

BELOW RIGHT: A Sprinter EMU of the Netherlands State Railways.

and in the growth of its suburban belt.

Technical developments in mechanical as well as electrical engineering also permitted the design and introduction of larger and more powerful cars, and the fusion of the tramway and railroad concepts allowed the introduction of high-speed intra-urban lines, which became typical of urban areas all over the world but especially in North America, where over 15,000 miles (24140km) of such line covered the continent.

By the 1920s the tramway situation was decidedly less rosy than it had been at the beginning of the century. Labour and materials were rising rapidly in cost and, as might have been expected, local and national politicians, voted into office by those who might suffer the economic consequences of fare increases, were unwilling to authorize the costlier tickets required to allow tramway managers to match expenditure with income. The problem here was that the systems resulting

from the initial capital investment were reaching the ends of their useful lives, and that the profits from the good years had not been retained by the city authorities for the renewal that would be the inevitable requirement of considerable use. Thus the maintenance of tramway systems was becoming increasingly expensive, there was insufficient capital for the large-scale renovations that were needed and, perhaps most threateningly of all, there was the prospect of declining markets as a result of the start of mass-production of motor cars and motor buses. The overall consequence of this concatenation of events was real competition for the tramway at a time when it was more viable in economic terms to introduce feeder bus services than to extend

the existing tramway systems to cater for the cities' continued growth.

Then came the great financial depression, which started in the U.S.A. during 1929 and soon spread to Europe. This effectively decimated the economies of most Western countries, in the process resulting in the swift collapse not only of many small-town tramways but also of the majority of intra-urban networks. Both of these were systems that operated at small profit margins, and were thus prone to the effects of competition. The motor bus effectively took over from the tramway, and from the early 1930s the trolley bus was in effect a way of killing off the tramway without wasting the electrical supply infrastructure which had been developed to

supply its power. There is some evidence that in the United States where municipal ownership was less common than in Europe, bus and oil companies tried to take over failing tramways so that the companies could replace them and so increase the profitability of both. It is perhaps ironic that this type of sharp business practice got its comeuppance within a little more than ten years as bus profitability disappeared in the face or the surge of private car ownership. Many municipalities had to intervene to ensure that at least the basic elements of a public transportation system remained.

Tramway managers did not give in without a considerable struggle, however. In the U.S.A. the President's Congress Committee of Streetcar Companies,

ABOVE LEFT: *An early British Columbia Electric Railway trolley in Vancouver, 1900. This open-air, double-truck car is on Westminster Avenue (now Main Street at 9th Avenue).*

ABOVE: *One of Victoria, British Columbia's first trolleys under the B.C.E.R. The photograph was taken in 1898 near Esquimalt Naval Station.*

ABOVE: B.C.E.R. Street Car 105 on a run from Harris (East Georgia) along Victoria Drive, via Georgia to Kitsilano Beach where the photograph was taken.

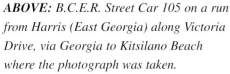

RIGHT: These B.C.E.R. electrically-powered units of decidedly strange appearance were created for the important task of track cleaning to ensure maximum traction without the interference of snow, leaves and other litter.

generally known as the PCC, undertook the research and sponsored the production of a new design of tram that would offer levels of comfort and performance equal to those of the private motor car. The result was the so-called PCC car, which staved off the closure of many tramway systems, and also saved many others, to form the basis of a revival of the tramway concept. Some of these are still operational, and indeed have become something of a grail for those fascinated by tramway heritage as an aspect of urban renewal. The PCC arrived in Europe late in the 1940s, and one of the first lines modified was the U.K.'s pioneering Blackpool Tramway: this was modernized with large numbers of trams built to the PCC concept, and so ensured

the system's survival up to the present.

Before this, the stringencies of World War II had hastened the decline of tramways in the U.K. and France, but at the same time created the opportunity for large-scale reconstruction in Belgium, the Netherlands, Germany and eastern Europe. In the U.K. the nationalization of municipal electrical supplies was another reason for the replacement of tramways by cheaper motor buses in much of the country, although some tramways, such as those of Glasgow and Liverpool, enjoyed a revival after World War II with new trams and reserved-track extensions, but never enough to ensure they became a dominant part of the network. The last city system to close in the U.K. was that of

Glasgow, which shut during 1962.

The 1960s constituted a decade of despair for the concept of public transport in many parts of the world. Most of those involved in industry and all types of traffic planning came to the belief that the motor car would become the standard form of transport for the majority of people, with buses only for those who could not afford cars, and that cities could somehow be adapted to cater for the increased levels of motor traffic that would result. By 1962, the only tramway system left in the U.K. was that of Blackpool, which had a reserved track along the sea front. A few tramway systems survived in North American cities, though the general belief was that it was only a matter of time before these last

ABOVE: Trams running along Des Voeux Road, Hong Kong.

LEFT: A brightly painted tram in Hong Kong.

OPPOSITE: Trams arriving and departing from Glasgow Central Station, Scotland.

vestiges of an earlier age fell to the apparently unstoppable surge of the motor car. In other parts of the world, planned or anticipated modernization of tramway systems came rapidly to a halt as costs rose in the aftermath of the disappearance from the tramway supply market of all types of mass-production economy.

The one stronghold of the tramway in this period was the mainland of the European continent. Here, in general, there was continued investment in the tramway, the largest commitments to the concept being those of the countries in the northern and eastern parts of the continent. Thus nations such as France, Italy and Spain proceeded toward the abandonment of the

tramway, while West Germany emerged as the main force in tramway development, in which the German manufacturer Düwag came to prominence as a designer of tramcars in general, and of articulated tramcars in particular. These latter could be operated by just one person, with most fares collected off the car by season ticket sales or ticket machines at stops.

This increase in the passenger/crew ratio was just one of the ways in which the operating economics of the tramcar were improved to the point at which the tramcar once again emerged and was financially superior to the bus. Moreover, despite an increase in car ownership, large-scale modernization of tramcar fleets and the

infrastructure over which they operated encouraged patronage, especially as passengers came to appreciate the advantages of travelling on a tramcar operating over reserved tracks. This was at a time when urban motor car transport was becoming increasingly slow as cities filled with cars all travelling in and out of the centre at the same basic times, and all needing somewhere to park in urban areas never designed for this type of congestion. In many city centres, most especially in Austria, Belgium and Germany, the tram was liberated from the worst effects of traffic congestion by the construction of shallow subway systems under busy crossroads and crowded streets.

Belgium, the Netherlands and the countries of eastern Europe became the home of the Europeanized PCC car, which attracted traffic by its high performance and frequent service. As the communist regimes of eastern Europe allowed little in the way of private car ownership, the availability of high-capacity public transport was of key importance. Full metro systems (known in the U.K. as underground railways) were unaffordable outside the major conurbations, so for many cities the tramway was the most important aspect of municipally-controlled urban transport. Centralized planning inevitably meant that the U.S.S.R. rapidly came to the position of the world's largest tramway operator, with

OPPOSITE LEFT: *A City of Birmingham tram at Pype Hayes Terminus, England.*

OPPOSITE RIGHT: *Streamlined double- and single-decker trams on the seafront at Blackpool, England.*

LEFT: *Trams operating in Johnston Road, Wanchai, in busy Hong Kong.*

Leningrad (once more known as St. Petersburg, as it had also been called up to 1914) possessing the largest tramway network. In the 1960s, the world's most prolific tramcar manufacturer was the Czechoslovak firm CKD Tatra of Prague. As communist-bloc economic agreement made it the supplier for most of Eastern Europe as well as the U.S.S.R., the company expanded its production facilities to the extent that it was delivering 1,000 cars per year, or almost three every day.

By the late 1960s, farther-sighted Western planners had begun to appreciate the disadvantages of massive reliance on the motor car and, as a result, a steady reduction in public transport. In some major

cities peak-time traffic congestion was reaching virtually 'gridlock' proportions, and this had resulted in an attempt to cater for the ever-increasing demands of motor car ownership by the creation of new mega-highways in urban areas: these could be created only by the destruction of vast construction paths through the cities in question, a process that divided communities both physically and economically and, as soon became apparent, resulted in major economic and social decline. This tendency was especially notable in the U.S.A. and, to a lesser extent, Canada. Many cities therefore saw a swift economic decline in their city centres as new shopping malls, reliant almost entirely on motor car transport, were created to fulfil the requirements of populations moving steadily from high-density housing in the city centre to low-density housing in the suburbs.

The social and economic ramifications of this process were not all that had now begun to worry the planners, however, for there were also increasing concerns about the environmental pollution inherent in the system. Therefore the planners and politicians decided to turn their eyes east across the Atlantic Ocean to see how the planners of Europe had overcome the problems to keep and indeed strengthen the flourishing nature of their city centres. An early appreciation of the European success was a need for an effective policy for low-cost public transport that could offer a very real alternative to the motor car by the high

average speed it could maintain along reserved-track tramways.

The consequent revival of the fortunes of the streetcar (otherwise the tram), usually within the context of a light rail vehicle, has been just as extraordinary in North America as it has been in Europe, and reflects the signal fact that while the Americans may not yet have overcome their fascination with the motor car, they have finally come to an appreciation that it is not feasible, either economically or socially, to rebuild their cities to allow unfettered use of the motor car. This appreciation has surfaced in many parts of the country, but is perhaps strongest in California with its sturdy if perhaps idiosyncratic approach to environmental matters.

As noted above, American planners started to look to Europe in the 1970s for concepts of the means they could employ to rescue their cities from outward-spreading decay and resultant economic decline. With urban transportation now owned by public bodies, the development of improved public transport could be undertaken with a combination of city, state and national resources. This situation arrived at much the same time as the end of the American involvement in the Vietnam War, which meant that the military manufacturers were beginning to look for different markets to keep their production capabilities working at maximum profitability after the curtailment of military equipment spending, and decided that public transport would rapidly become the scene of considerable growth. An initial consequence of this

OPPOSITE ABOVE: Trams safely share the streets with pedestrians in Russia.

OPPOSITE BELOW: Copenhagen's suburban S-Bahn.

THIS PAGE
RIGHT: Amtrak AEM7 No. 905 at Harrison Station, New Jersey with the Metroliner services from New York and Washington, D.C.

BELOW LEFT and RIGHT: Amtrak Metroliners used in the North-East Corridor between Boston and Washington, D.C.

LEFT: In small and densely populated countries such as Belgium, an efficient network of commuter and rapid transport systems is rightly appreciated as a vital tool in the easing of road traffic congestion and the timely movement of passengers in urban environments.

BELOW: As one of the hub nations of continental Europe and, just as importantly, of the European Union, Belgium has sensibly made its main-line railroad network an intrinsic element of the northern European system so that its services can travel into neighbouring countries as well as the services of other countries passing into Belgium or even through it.

situation was that Boston and San Francisco, two cities still operating tramway systems, contracted with Boeing-Vertol for the production of new LRVs (light rail vehicles) of the articulated type. These were based on a design schemed as the basis for an LRV which the company hoped would emulate the PCC of some 40 years earlier in becoming standard throughout the U.S.A. and also offering considerable export potential. The company's hopes were sound but its product was not, and the LRV was a disaster at the technical level as the company sought to 'reinvent the wheel' rather than learning from the wealth of experience available from practical operations elsewhere.

Thus it was in Canada that the first successful development of the new type of LRV emerged in North America, for it was here the city Edmonton decided that rather than create a wholly new concept it would draw on the experience of current European success and therefore opt for the alternative approach of adapting European technology to the North American situation. The city thus constructed a new light rail line, partly on redundant railroad alignment and partly in city subways, and from 1978 used this for the operation of Siemens-Düwag trams imported from West Germany. The system was immediately successful, and as such was rapidly adopted as the model for San Diego in the U.S.A. and Calgary in Canada. In these two cities, it was decided that the creation of subways would be too expensive, so pedestrian and transit precincts were established in the city

LEFT: A suburban electric trainset built by Soreframe under a Budd licence for the Portuguese State Railways, seen here on the Cascais line.

BELOW: A Class 4020 EMU of the Austrian State Railways, late 1970s.

centres, it being rightly appreciated that trams, being guided pollution-free vehicles, could be operated successfully and safely in areas otherwise reserved for pedestrians.

The success of these systems in attracting back to the use of public transit large numbers of motor car owners, who would never have considered the use of a bus, led to a considerable expansion in both the development and construction of light rail systems, and this has continued right up to the present. Major cities such as Baltimore, Buffalo, Dallas, Denver, Los Angeles, Portland, Sacramento and St. Louis have built new light rail lines, many of them as part of systems that are still expanding geographically, and is scheduling to meet the demand engendered by their success. More recent examples of new and emerging systems are to be found in Jersey City and Salt Lake City, and progress toward similar systems has been made in other cities such as New York and Seattle. Moreover, the success of the concept persuaded cities such as Cleveland, Pittsburgh and Philadelphia, which operated systems based on the earlier streetcar concept, to invest in the new type of rolling stock and begin a programme of expansion.

The example of Los Angeles is notably important, for this was an urban area that discarded its trams and intra-urbans during the 1960s in the belief that the city could live and breathe with the motor car. The dense pollution that has become a characteristic feature of Los Angeles finally proved to the city fathers that their predecessors were wholly wrong, and the

ABOVE: *The Metro maintenance depot in Rio de Janeiro, Brazil.*

RIGHT: *A suburban EMU in Rio de Janeiro on the approach to Don Pedro Station.*

OPPOSITE: *Four different-style EMUs on the approach to Don Pedro Station in Rio de Janeiro, Brazil.*

city has inaugurated two new light rail lines, with a third already under construction.

Farther to the south, Mexico is a country in which the blight of the motor car has in places reached a situation even more acute than that of the worst of the American cities, and a similar approach has been belatedly adopted. As a result there are new light rail lines in Guadalajara, Monterey and, most significantly of all, the huge conurbation of Mexico City. Tramways had virtually disappeared from South America by the end of the 1960s, but the first new light rail lines have now appeared in Buenos Aires and Rio de Janeiro.

Light rail first came into existence on the mainland of Europe in the form of new rolling stock and track segregated from public roadways to ensure that the services could maintain a high average speed. The pioneering concept of the European light rail system was derived largely from the planning which took place in the Swedish city of Gothenburg where, during a period of some 15 years, an ordinary city street tramway was extended through the suburbs, both new and existing, on high-speed reserved track, and every possible incentive was used to persuade the public to make extensive use of public transport. The existing rolling stock gave way to high-performance trams, and traffic restrictions were imposed to give priority to trams in the central area. This Swedish system was created without the cost of building tunnels, in the process not only minimizing cost but at the same time keeping public transport

on the surface as an attractive and readily accessible system.

Many other cities in other parts of the world have adopted the same concept since 1980: just in Europe, for example, in Austria there are Graz and Linz, in Belgium there is Ghent, in the Netherlands there is Amsterdam, and in Switzerland there are Basle and Zürich. These fine examples are matched slightly differently in other Austrian, Belgian and German cities, where in general it was thought that the best way of improving the average speed of public transport in city streets was to provide a segregated path in subways: examples of this approach are to be found in cities such as Antwerp, Brussels, Hanover, Köln, Stuttgart and Vienna. However, the growing capital cost of underground work has begun to make this type of operation prohibitively expensive, and as a result there has emerged a swing back to the concept of road traffic restrictions to provide public transport with priority.

LEFT and OPPOSITE: A Class 1042 *electric locomotive heading an Austrian State Railways express train on the Semmering Line.*

The creation of these new and upgraded systems has led to the establishment of a novel terminology to help differentiate such systems from ordinary tramways, and Supertram, Light Rail, Metro, Sneltrom (express tram) and Stadtbahn (town rail) are just some of the names now used, and a number of upgraded subway tramways in Germany are marketed in the same way as underground metros by using the term U-Bahn (underground railroad). It is worth noting that a feature which did much to enhance the popularity of the subway during the 1970s and 1980s was that it offered the possibility of level boarding of high-floor cars in the city suburbs. On surface lines in the suburbs, there was often space available to install platforms level with the vehicle floor, which made the vehicles readily accessible for passengers in wheelchairs or those with prams and buggies; in other parts of the system the vehicles use fold-down steps.

Apart from the public desire for the creation or revitalization of light rail systems as a means of cutting down the pollution and increasingly slow speed of private motor car transport in city centres, the primary driving force for the urban transport revolution was the mass of legislation enacted during the 1960s to lay the groundwork for progress towards the new era in public transport. As a result of this legislation, local authorities were allocated the task of developing plans for integrated transport systems, and in the major conurbations, PTEs (Passenger Transport Executives) were established to assume responsibility for the development and operation of public transport in their areas.

One of the first PTEs to make progress was the Tyne & Wear PTE, located in the heavily industrialized and heavily populated north-west of England, which launched its public transport plan in 1973. This proposed the establishment of a light rail system to take over the alignment of 26 miles (42km) of run-down local railway track that were to be connected into 8.5 miles (13.5km) of new infrastructure to create a network of electrified suburban lines as the heart of an integrated passenger transport system. The initial route was opened in stages between 1980 and 1984 and, as the U.K.'s first modern light rail system, with a capacity of more than 40 million passengers per year, was largely successful in one of its primary tasks of assisting in the regeneration of Tyneside.

In London, a key issue in the planned regeneration of the docklands area east of the city was public transport. The light rail concept was deemed appropriate and affordable in this context, and was adopted during 1982. The initial 7-mile (12-km) system was then extended to 13 miles (21km), and is now being further extended to the region south of the Thames river. The network has proved very popular, and more than 22 million passengers per year are carried. Many of the U.K.'s major cities are planning to use a range of systems, from segregated and automated operation (on former rail alignments) to conventional street tramways.

LEFT: An intermediate-level compartment at the end of a TATOA double-deck commuter coach on Toronto's GO Rapid Transit System.

BELOW : Exterior of Toronto's GO Rapid Transit System.

During the 1990s new technology has been developed to provide low-floor trams with step-free entrances only 13.75in (0.35m) above rail level. Surface systems achieved exactly the same effect just by building up kerbs slightly to create a matching height. This is now the favoured solution for improving the accessibility of trams, and over 2,000 low-floor cars have been delivered or ordered for European systems. In the U.K. all new systems are required to offer step-free access to trams, resulting in new rolling stock which will be supplied from manufacturers in Belgium, Germany and Italy.

In countries such as France, Italy and Spain which, like the U.K., had abandoned their tramway heritage, there has also been a resurgence of interest in the tram. France has introduced new systems in cities such as Grenoble, Nantes, Paris and Rouen, and comparable systems are in the offing for Bordeaux, Montpellier, Orléans and Toulon. The Spanish city of Valencia has similarly built a new tramway and other cities are developing plans for improved public transport. In Italy, Genoa has a new segregated light rail line and many cities are planning tramway systems with the support of companies.

The tram as used in Australia and New Zealand was based closely on its British counterpart, although double-deck vehicles were less frequent as a reflection of the less cramped conditions typical of antipodean cities. There was a rapid decline of the tram concept in the 1950s and 1960s as small-town systems were terminated for economic

Several new extensions have been constructed and two local rail lines have been converted to light rail operation and linked by street operation with the city centre.

The return of trams to Sydney, Melbourne's great Australian rival, occurred in 1997 with the opening of a short line built and operated by the private sector. This was designed as the basis of an expanded network, including operation in city streets, to be largely completed by the time the Olympic Games are held in the city in the year 2000. Elsewhere, Brisbane is considering the introduction of trams and the surviving route in Adelaide is scheduled for modernization. This line was due for extension in the 1980s, but a change of political power saw the introduction of the German type of O-Bahn guided bus-way system.

Trams had disappeared from the city streets of New Zealand's major cities by the

ABOVE: *Bombardier's LRC (Light, Rapid and Comfortable) train operated by VIA Rail, Canada.*

RIGHT: *Netherlands State Railways three-car train set, in the late 1970s.*

reasons, while at the same time cities such as Adelaide, Brisbane and Sydney sacrificed their trams for industrial and political reasons. However, the southern hemisphere's largest system, some 137 miles (220km) long, is that of Melbourne, which survived intact thanks to good management and political support. The system's first new trams for 20 years arrived in 1975, and since that year the arrival of more than 350 more new cars has transformed the system from a very traditional and conservative operation to one that is much more customer-orientated.

*OPPOSITE: The Docklands Light
Railway, serving the East End of London.*

THIS PAGE
*RIGHT: A tram in Nicholson Street,
Melbourne, Australia.*

*BELOW: Docklands 42 and 57 arriving at
Poplar, bound for Stratford, East London.*

1960s. The year 1995 saw their return to Christchurch in the form of a heritage loop through the city centre using museum cars to provide a service aimed mainly at tourists. The construction of light rail systems are also being planned for Auckland and Wellington.

Japan has in general suffered even more than the U.S.A. and Europe from the effects of massed private cars, so local conditions were not good for the short-term survival of the street tramway. However, many surviving tramways have now been upgraded to run on segregated track. These form the basis of a substantial network of light railways that are an important part of the well-used public transport network. Ironically, some small-town street tramway operations have survived and are currently being modernized, and the first low-floor tram, based on a German design, was introduced in 1997. Elsewhere in Asia, rail-based urban public transport is less common. Located in Calcutta, India's only surviving tramway is a substantial network, but years of poor investment have left services in a precarious state. By contrast Manila, the capital of the Philippines, opened a new segregated light rail line across the city in 1984, and the success of this system has encouraged the construction of two more lines using private capital. The North Korean capital of Pyongyang has built a new tramway system and in Malaysia a new light metro system opened in 1996.

China had little tramway operation. In 1997, however, it regained the ex-British colony of Hong Kong, where British-style double-deck trams have run since 1904, and these continue to compete successfully with intensive bus operation on the streets of Hong Kong island. A complete contrast is the 20-mile (32-km) long light rail system, built since 1988, in the suburban township of Tuen Mun. This is one of the most heavily patronized rail systems in the world and carries over 112 million passengers every year.

In Africa the light rail concept is limited to Tunisia and Egypt. Tunis has created a 20-mile (32-km) system since 1985 with German-built articulated cars operating on four surface lines that carry 90 million passengers a year. Alexandria has a street tramway and a suburban light rail line, while Cairo, Heliopolis and Helwan operate modernized light rail lines.

The concept of the light rail system is not of rigid definition, but in effect was conceived to accommodate all types of tracked transport in the gap between the bus and the heavy metro, or conventional railway, and can be operated like any of them. A light rail system is costlier to make than any bus system on city streets, but for a given capacity can be cheaper to operate, has lower whole-life costs, offers a higher

average speed, produces less pollution, and in general is more successful in attracting motorists to public transport. In comparison with a metro or urban railway, a light rail system is cheaper to build and operate but operates at a lower speed. Among its other advantages, however, are the fact that it offers a visible example of successful public transport, provides better penetration of urban areas, is typified by better security, and generates less noise. Light rail can cater

economically and effectively for passenger flows between 2,000 and 20,000 passengers an hour, and as a result is usually to be found in cities with populations between 200,000 and 1 million.

The light rail concept is usually based on the use of steel-wheeled vehicles running on steel rails and collecting electrical power from an overhead wire. Diesel light rail is a concept that has been evaluated to only a limited extent, and may

ABOVE: A key element in the success of rapid transit systems in busy urban areas is the use of double-decked cars which can carry more passengers on a given number of axles.

OPPOSITE: Another vital aspect of systems such as the Metrolink, is the layout of stations with extensive car parking facilities and platforms which optimize the rapid movement of passengers.

prove to be useful for low-cost starter lines that can then be adapted to the full light rail concept. The steel rails can be grooved so that they lie flush with a street surface, or may be ballasted like normal railroad track, and this capability makes light rail the only system that can operate on both city streets and jointly with conventional rail services. It also offers the possibility of extending regional railroad services to the city centre by way of transfer points from rail to street track. This notion, adopted with very considerable success in the German city of Karlsruhe with dual-voltage light rail vehicles, is now extending to other cities.

Light rail is also very flexible in its applications, and can thus operate in a wide range of built-up environments. It can serve as a tramway in the street, though maximization of its advantages over the bus requires the minimization of unsegregated street track. Within public streets the track can be segregated by any of several means. The track can be laid in tarmac, concrete, ballast or even grass according to the operational and environmental needs of the whole system. Light rail can be built on previous railroad alignments, or indeed share track with the railroad in the form of little-used freight lines or those with limited passenger services, and technical progress means that the required safety arrangements are readily available for mixed services.

A topic closely related to the light rail revolution is the re-emergence of commuter trains, sometimes called heavy rail to differentiate it from light rail, as an important aspect of urban regeneration, for

LEFT: *A surburban double-deck EMU runs into Milsons Point Station after crossing the Sydney Harbour Bridge, Australia.*

BELOW: *A double-deck EMU on surburban service halts at Central Station, Sydney.*

while the light rail system is dedicated to the rapid movement of people between various points in the urban environment, the commuter rail system has been re-established as the most cost-effective means of moving the work force into the urban environment at the beginning of the working day and then returning the same people to their homes outside the city at the end of the day. The commuter train never wholly died in the U. S.A., but was severely strained by the rivalry of the private motor car between the 1950s and 1980s and declined to a very low technical and commercial level.

In recent years, however, there has been a considerable renaissance in commuter operations in the U.S.A.'s major cities, and in a growing number of these conurbations the regional authorities have taken to operating what may be termed 'heavy rail' commuter services with their own trains running on track either acquired or leased from the railroad companies; in a number of other conurbations the regional authorities have contracted with the local railroad company for the operation of heavy rail services.

In the area covered by the Connecticut Department of Transportation, for instance, a contract has been signed with Amtrak for the operation of a 50.6-mile (81.4-km) *Shoreline East* commuter service between

New London and New Haven via six intermediate stations. The service was launched in 1990 with two EMD 'F7M'-class locomotives and Pullman Standard cars dating from the 1950s and bought from the Port Authority of Allegheny County, Pittsburgh, following the latter's termination of its own commuter services. The Connecticut Department of Transportation has since expanded the operation by leasing from Guildford two 'GP38'- and one 'GP7W'-class power cars to haul 10 Bombardier Comet cars, supplemented by 11 existing Budd 8SPV200 railcars remodelled by Amtrak's Wilmington facility as standard cars.

At the start of 1996 the service was organized on the basis of peak-time schedules during the working week with two reciprocal runnings to ensure that the trains were positioned correctly for peak times. During 1996 the traffic carried increased by 6.5 per cent and, in anticipation of the high track speeds expected from Amtrak's forthcoming electrification of the line, an order was placed for six 3,000-hp (2237-kW) diesel locomotives to be manufactured by AMF Technotransport. The Connecticut Department of Transportation also controls (and with the New York Department of Transportation jointly subsidizes to the extent of 60 per cent of the operating deficit and 63 per cent of the capital cost) the commuter services operated by Metro-North between the city of New York and New Haven. The Connecticut Department of Transportation has also pressed the case

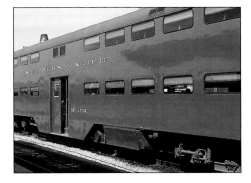

ABOVE: A stainless-steel Rock Island Railroad coach No.150 on commuter services out of La Salle Street Station, Chicago to Vermont Street.

ABOVE RIGHT: Southern Pacific double-deck suburban coach in San Francisco Station.

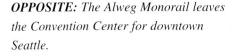

OPPOSITE: The Alweg Monorail leaves the Convention Center for downtown Seattle.

for bus shuttles to its stations, thereby promoting reverse commuting, and such services now operate in Greenwich, New Haven, Norwalk and Stamford.

The Long Island Rail Road Company, which is a wholly-owned subsidiary of the Metropolitan Transportation Authority, an agency of the State of New York, operates commuter services between the city of New York and destinations on Long Island, and operates within the limits of a budget allocated by the Metropolitan Transit Authority and including a sizeable element of capital investment in new rolling stock, station improvements and general infrastructure maintenance.

The extent and nature of the system's operations is revealed by the fact that in 1996 it carried 73.6 million passengers, and this was the fourth year in succession that the number of passengers had increased. However, in the first part of 1996 a reverse trend became evident, probably as a result of a fare increase of almost 10 per cent.

The Long Island Rail Road's services reach out into the Long Island counties of Nassau and Suffolk as well as to certain parts of the eastern Queens part of the New

York conurbation. The services had nine branch lines that converge onto three main stations in New York, namely Penn Station, Flatbush Avenue in Brooklyn and Hunters Point Avenue that is open only at peak hours and served only by diesel trains: the bulk of the daily traffic is handled by Penn Station, in the form of 208,000 passengers, the other two stations handling 40,000 passengers between them. It is worth noting that the Long Island Rail Road also handles a large quantity of freight services.

By the middle of the 1990s the Long Island Rail Road's programme to improve Penn Station was well under way, the $190 million programme being designed to better the access to and the movement within the station, as well as to improve the station's facilities in terms of the level of comfort and information for the passengers. This effort is reflected in the fact that the average passenger now has 20 per cent more space and a 40 per cent increase in access points, the latter including five stairways, three escalators, five elevators to Long Island Rail Road platforms, and even a new entrance. The importance attached to the attraction of commuter travellers back to the train (there are now 42 rather than the original 36 train movements per hour) is also revealed by general enhancements such as improvements of the signs and master destination board, a new public address system, more effective lighting, and a traveller concourse with seats and washroom facilities.

The Long Island Rail Road started to receive new rolling stock in 1997–98, but

up to that time operated a fleet of locomotives comprising 28 2,000-hp (1491-kW) 'GP36-2' class, 23 1,500-hp (1119-kW) 'MP15AC' class and three 'FL9AC'-class units as primary haulers, and also eight 1,000-hp (746-kW) 'SW1001' units for shunting operations. Passengers are carried in a fleet of 1,125 cars including 760 'M1'-class multiple-unit cars on the electrified inner suburban lines of the city of New York and in Nassau and Suffolk counties, and 174 examples of the 'M3'-class car obtained in the mid-1980s. Operations to other parts of the network are handled by trains hauled by diesel-electric locomotives, which are scheduled for early replacement in the railroad's major reinvestment programme. The Long Island Rail Road also has an eye open to the use of more flexible technology in the future, and is therefore evaluating dual-mode (diesel and third-rail electric) traction. The operator runs a single train in each direction during the peak-hour period between Penn Station and Port Jefferson on a non-electrified line using some of its 10 prototype double-deck cars obtained from Mitsui in Japan and powered by two FL9AC-class locomotives rebuilt to their current configuration by Adtranz, or ABB Traction as it then was.

It was in March 1995 that the Long Island Rail Road signed contracts worth some $250 million for new locomotives and passenger cars. The bulk of the contracts' value went to General Electric for 23 examples of its 'DE30AC'-class diesel-electric locomotives for push/pull

OPPOSITE: A Chicago & North Western Railroad suburban train with double-deck coaches leaving Chicago.

RIGHT: Class F40PH locomotives 236, 355 and 353 on the eastbound California Zephyr *coming down the Denver & Rio Grande tracks through Price River Canyon just above Helper, Utah.*

operations, as well as options for another 23 units that could be all of the same type or alternatively eight of the same type and 15 of a revised dual-mode type. The contracts also covered the manufacture and delivery of 48 new passenger cars. By this time research had revealed that passengers had a decided preference for 2+2 seating rather than the 2+3 arrangement typical of the 10 prototype cars that had been initially evaluated over a two-year period with maximum accommodation for 180 passengers. The order therefore comprises cars with provision for a maximum of 145 passengers, reduced to 139 passengers in cab cars.

Farther to the south along the eastern seaboard of the U.S.A. is the area covered by the Maryland Mass Transit Administration's Maryland Rail Commuter Service. This provides services over the 75.6-mile (121.6-km) route linking Washington, D.C. and Perryville via Baltimore on electrified track within the context of Amtrak's 'North-East Corridor' operation, a 37.9-mile (61-km) route

linking Washington, D.C. and Baltimore on non-electrified track, and a 72.6-mile (116.8-km) route linking Washington, D.C. and Martinsburg on non-electrified track. The service between Washington and Perryville is the responsibility of four electric locomotives hauling Japanese-built passenger cars, while the services on the other two routes are operated with older stock using diesel locomotives.

During 1994 the Maryland Rail Commuter Service posted a total annual passenger figure of some 5 millions which, at 6 per cent over the previous year, seemed to indicate a levelling off of growth from the 20 per cent figure evident in previous years. Operating within the context of the Maryland Mass Transit Authority, the Maryland Rail Commuter Service is able to offer tickets and passes valid throughout the

system and this is clearly a decided inducement to passengers to use all aspects of Maryland Mass Transit, which include the bus, light rail and metro services of Baltimore and, it is hoped for the near future, Washington, D.C. The Maryland Rail Commuter Service is growing slightly with the aid of a federal financial package that is allowing a 13.4-mile (21.6-km) extension to Frederick with the aid of new track, signalling equipment, rolling stock, etc. Further evidence of the integrated nature of the Maryland Mass Transit Authority's nature is provided by the Maryland Rail Commuter Service's completion of a new station at Dorsey, which has a major parking capability at its own links to the Maryland state highway system.

The Maryland Rail Commuter Service's train equipment comprises four 'AEM7'-class electric locomotives and 25 3,000-hp (2238-kW) 'GP40WH-2'-class locomotives, together with more than 100 passenger cars in the form of 43 refurbished New Jersey Transit Authority and 63 new Sumitomo cars, complemented in due course by 50 double-deck cars ordered in 1995 from Kawasaki.

Located farther to the north, around Boston, the Massachusetts Bay Transportation Authority provides commuter rail services on 11 routes into Boston on a network comprising 308.1 miles (495.9 km) of track originally owned up to the 1970s by Penn Central and Boston & Maine. From 1988 the Massachusetts Bay Transportation Authority's sphere of influence was extended by the inauguration of a service to Providence, Rhode Island, on Amtrak tracks. All of the Massachusetts Bay Transportation Authority's services are operated under contract by Amtrak.

The Massachusetts Bay Transportation Authority controls an integrated and comprehensive local and regional transportation system based on four metro lines, five light rail lines, four trolley bus

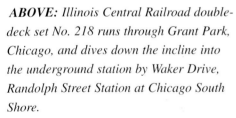

ABOVE: *Illinois Central Railroad double-deck set No. 218 runs through Grant Park, Chicago, and dives down the incline into the underground station by Waker Drive, Randolph Street Station at Chicago South Shore.*

ABOVE RIGHT: *Chicago elevated railroad train about to cross the bridge over the platform ends of the Chicago & North Western Railroad Station. F unit No. 424 waits on the right.*

OPPOSITE: *Milwaukee Road Railroad Push-Pull arrives at Union Station by the Chicago river.*

and 155 bus routes, all operating within the same basic fare system to encourage interconnection between various elements of the overall system, which also includes the 'heavy rail' commuter system. In 1995 the Massachusetts Bay Transportation Authority recorded a passenger total of 23 million, and further expansion of the commuter service is imminent from the inauguration of a 22.9-mile (36.8-km) extension from Framingham to Worcester on the western side of the network south of the line to Fitchburg, and from the start in the later 1990s of 'Old Colony Railroad' services along three routes to Kingston, Middleboro and Scituate to the south-east of Boston and including 21 new stations. These latter extensions of the network are

estimated to result in the delivery of up to 15,000 more passengers per day to the South Station in Boston. The success of the Massachusetts Bay Transportation Authority in schedule-keeping, fare management and general efficiency has led to the local decision to consider other extensions to the route network to both the north and south of Boston, including coastal destinations such as Newburyport and Greenbush.

The Massachusetts Bay Transportation Authority operates its services with 58 diesel locomotives and 420 passenger cars. The diesel locomotives include 25 'F40PH-2C' bought from General Motors, and 18 'F40PH' and 12 'F40PH-2M'-class units rebuilt to an improved standard by

Morrison Knudsen. Further capability is being provided, largely for the Worcester and Old Colony services, by the delivery of 25 more locomotives remanufactured to an upgraded standard by AMF Technotransport. The passenger cars are of mixed origins and include 67 units made by Messerschmitt-Bölkow-Blohm in West Germany, 147 units fabricated by Bombardier in Canada, 92 double-deck units constructed by Kawasaki in Japan, and 58 Pullman Standard units originally made in the U.S.A. and now upgraded.

Much farther to the east, Metra is the name of the commuter branch of the Chicago Regional Transportation Authority under the overall supervision of North-East Illinois Regional Commuter Railroad

Corporation's Chicago Commuter Rail Service Board, this mass of nomenclature finally revealing that Metra is in fact the organization that operates commuter rail services to and from the Chicago conurbation. The Metra system covers the six north-eastern counties of Illinois, and its extent of some 500 miles (805km) of route (including 1,200 miles/1930km of track) includes elements operated under contract by the Burlington Northern Santa Fe Railroad (originally the Burlington Northern Railroad, one route) and the Union Pacific Railroad (formerly the Chicago & North Western Railroad, three routes) on their own track but with Metra-owned equipment. Owned and operated by Metra itself are the track and equipment of the former Illinois Central, Milwaukee Road and Rock Island Railroads, and Metra has also leased the Norfolk Southern line to Orland Park for its South-West Service. Metra additionally operates two *Central Heritage Corridor* services in each direction between Chicago and Joliet.

During August 1998 Metra introduced a commuter service to the 52.8-mile (85-km) Wisconsin Central route linking Franklin Park (on Metra's own route between Chicago and Elgin) and Antioch via nine intermediate stations. Further extensions of the system are under active consideration.

Metra's rolling stock in the closing stages of 1995 included 137 diesel locomotives, 165 electric railcars and 700 passenger cars. The most important of the diesel locomotives were 28 3,200-hp (2386-kW) F40PH class, 86 3,200-hp (2386-kW) 'F40PH-2' class, 15 3,200-hp (2386-kW) 'F40C' class and 30 3,200-hp (2386-kW) 'F40PHM-2'-class units, while the most important types of electric railcar were the 150-passenger 'MA3A' class of which 130 were in service and the 150-passenger 'MA3B' class of which 35 were in service. Entering service since 1994 have been a number of 'highliner' electric multiple-unit cars after their reconstruction with full accessibility to physically handicapped passengers by Morrison Knudsen and later by Amerail.

Back on the east coast between Massachusetts and Maryland is the state of New Jersey, and this is the area of commuter train responsibility exercised by the organization known as New Jersey Transit Rail Operations Inc., which carries an annual total of some 42.7 million passengers over a system that comprises nine routes into Hoboken, Newark and the city of New York, and is operated with an integrated fare system to facilitate interchange within the various elements of the whole complex. Within this complex, New Jersey Transit Rail Operations owns much of the infrastructure (the other parts being in the hands of Amtrak and Conrail), all its own rolling stock and 145 stations.

The system operates some 600 services on every day of the working week, and these services fall into several distinct sectors. On the Jersey Coast line between Penn Station in New York and Bay Head there are *Jersey Arrow* services operated by electric multiple-units as far south as Long Branch, and also diesel-hauled services as

far as Bay Head. On the North-East Corridor from Penn Station to Trenton (and including the branch line to Princeton) there is another *Arrow* service also operated by electric multiple-units. From Newark extends the line into the Raritan Valley as far as Hackettstown operated by General Motors electric units, while the Morris and Essex lines are generally operated by electric multiple-units together with a number of diesel-hauled trains. Diesel services are standard on the services to Boonton, the Pascack Valley and Port Jervis, and the link to Atlantic City via Philadelphia is served by a fleet of five diesel locomotives and 18 passenger cars.

At the end of 1995 New Jersey Transit Rail Operations had 78 diesel-electric and 28 electric locomotives together with 300

OPPOSITE ABOVE: *A New Jersey Transit Authority EMU No. 1521 crosses the Passaic River into Newark Station on service from Penn Central Station, New York.*

OPPOSITE BELOW: *Another New Jersey Transit Authority EMU bound for Penn Central Station, runs through Harrison, New Jersey.*

RIGHT: *A classic Pennsylvania GG1 locomotive runs through Harrison, New Jersey with a New Jersey Transit train bound for Penn Central Station, New York.*

electric multiple-units and 389 passenger cars. The most numerous of the diesel-electric units were 13 3,000-hp (2238-kW) 'GP40PH-2'-class and 40 3,000-hp (2238-kW) 'F40PH-2'-class locomotives: the electric locomotives were 20 5,795-hp (4320-kW) 'ALP44'- and eight 6,000-hp (4475-kW) 'E60CP'-class units, and the primary electric multiple-units were 68 'MA1G'-class units in married pairs, 182 'MA1J'-class units in married pairs and 29 MA1J-class units in single cars. Recent additions have included another 17 ALP44-class electric locomotives to replace E60CP units, and the first Bombardier cars to replace older MA1G-class electric multiple-units.

On the other side of the U.S.A., operating in the extreme south of California on the west coast, is the North San Diego County Transit Development Board, which in 1995 started the *Coaster* service operated under contract by Amtrak over the 41.75-mile (67.2-km) route linking San Diego and Oceanside. This service runs over part of the 83.3 miles (134km) of route that the North San Diego County Transit authority bought from the Burlington Northern Santa Fe Railroad and includes the branch line between Oceanside and Escondido which is under consideration for a light rail service. The North San Diego County Transit Development Board has upgraded the route of the *Coaster* service in a number of ways, including six new stations and two upgraded stations, and for its service (comprising five trains to/from San Diego and one train to/from Oceanside in the

morning and evening of each day of the working week) five 'F40PHM-2C'-class diesel-electric locomotives and 16 double-deck coaches (eight cab cars and eight passenger cars) supplied by Bombardier and being supplemented by another five coaches.

Farther to the north along the Californian coast is the region in which there operates the Southern California Regional Rail Authority in and around the Los Angeles conurbation. It is planned that this system will eventually cover some 400 miles (645km), and the first three lines came into service during October 1992 after the Southern California Regional Rail Authority had purchased 338 miles (544km) of route from the Burlington Northern Santa Fe Railroad as the beginning of a programme designed to bring effective commuter services to five counties in the Los Angeles region. The

services introduced in 1992 operated under the designation 'Metrolink', and comprised the routes linking the Union Station in Los Angeles with Moorpark (the Ventura Line), Montclair (the San Bernardino Line), and Santa Clarita (the Santa Clarita Line), and two services added in 1995 were the Riverside Line on Union Pacific track and the Orange County Line, the latter extending to Oceanside and a link with service to San Diego. Further expansion came in October 1995 when the Metrolink network was extended to include the route between Irvine and Riverside via Santa Ana and Anaheim, so by the beginning of 1996 the Metrolink network comprised 338 miles (544km) of route with 42 stations, and during its first three years of service carried steadily increasing numbers of passengers, peaking in the year up to October 1995 at

4.4 million, a 33 per cent increase over the previous 12-month period.

The Metrolink services are operated by Amtrak, as noted above, using 23 'F59PH'-class and eight 'F59PHI'-class locomotives optimized for the type of low emissions now considered absolutely vital for all traffic operating in the heavily polluted Los Angeles basin, and 94 double-deck

passenger cars delivered by Bombardier. The operator was also to have received 26 special 'California Cars' ordered from Morrison Knudsen, but the order for these commuter cars was later cancelled because of manufacturing problems, and Metrolink instead leased more Bombardier cars from GO Transit of Canada.

There are several other commuter or

'heavy rail' operators in the U.S.A. filling the specialized niche between the 'light rail' systems of the city centres and the main-line services still running passenger and freight services between the U.S.A.'s main centres of population, but the above pen picture provides an encapsulated view of the overall nature of such services in the U.S.A.

OPPOSITE: A PATH (Port Authority Trans-Hudson) train from Newark, New Jersey to the World Trade Center, New York, halts at Harrison to pick up passengers.

RIGHT: A PATH train on service from the World Trade Center comes over the Passaic river into Newark, New Jersey.

Picture Acknowledgements
Amtrak: page 39 below left and
right
Austrian State Railways: pages
41 below, 44, 45
**Baltimore & Ohio Railroad
Museum:* page 12
Bek, Prague: page 10
Belgian State Railways: pages 31
above, 40 both
C.F.C.L./Image Select: pages 9, 52
Danish State Railways: page 38
below
General Electric: page 13 right
Hawker Siddeley, Canada: page
46 both
Hsinhua News Agency: page 21
above left and right
**New York, New Haven &
Hartford Railroad:** page 8
Netherlands State Railways:
pages 31 below, 47 below
**Norwegian State Railways,
Oslo:** page 30
Portuguese State Railways: page
41 above
**©Railfotos, Millbrook House
Limited, Oldbury, W. Midlands,
England:** pages 34 below, 35, 36
left, 38 above, 39 above, 54, 55
both. H. Ballantine: pages 4–5, 11,
14, 16, 18, 19 both, 20, 22, 23, 24,
25, 26 both, 28, 29 both, 34 top,
37, 48, 49 both. P.J. Howard: pages
42, 43 both, 53, 57, 58, 59
both, 60 both, 61, 62, 63.
G.W. Morrison: pages 7, 15, 17, 21
below, 27, 36 right, 50, 51.
J.B. Snell: page 56
Swiss Federal Railways: page 13
left
Vancouver Rapid Transport:
pages 32 and 33 all
Via Rail, Canada: page 47 above
Wuppertaler Stadtwerke: page 2

** Prints/transparencies through
Military Archives & Research
Services, Lincolnshire, England.*